# PROBLEM SOLVING
# Step by Step

**Metropolitan Teaching and Learning Company**
33 Irving Place
New York, New York 10003

Cover photographs: Zeffa-Craddock/The Stock Market
Printed in the United States of America

ISBN: 1-58120-701-8
10 9 8 7 6 5 4 3

# STEP 1 • Table of Contents

# STEP I • Topics

## Tables
6.1 Reading a Table
6.2 Making a Table

## Graphs
1.2 Reading a Picture Graph
5.2 Reading a Bar Graph

## Other Visual Displays
1.1 Using a Picture
2.2 Using a Picture
3.2 Using a Picture
4.1 Using a Number Line
5.1 Using a Number Line
7.1 Reading a Schedule
7.2 Reading a Calendar
9.1 Looking for a Pattern

## Answer Interpretation
1.3 Underlining the Question
4.2 Is the Answer a Word or a Number?
6.3 Is the Answer a Word or a Number?
11.2 Deciding Which Unit to Use
11.3 Not Enough Information

## Visual Thinking
2.1 Acting It Out
3.1 Acting It Out
7.3 Using Coins
8.1 Drawing a Picture
8.2 Using a Number Line
8.3 Acting It Out
9.2 Drawing a Picture
10.1 Drawing a Picture
10.2 Acting It Out
11.1 Drawing a Picture
12.1 Using Dimes and Pennies

## Recognizing Important Information
3.4 Using Number Sense
5.3 Deciding Whether to Add
  or Subtract
10.3 Underlining Needed Information
12.2 Underlining Needed Information

## Algebraic Thinking
2.3 Writing a Number Sentence
3.3 Writing a Number Sentence

Name _____

# Using a Picture

How many  are there?

**A.** Find a  in the picture .

**B.** Put a ✔ on each  .

**C.** Count the  as you ✔. _____

## Put a ✔ and count.
## Write how many.

1. _____

2. _____

4. _____

3. _____

● Numbers to 12

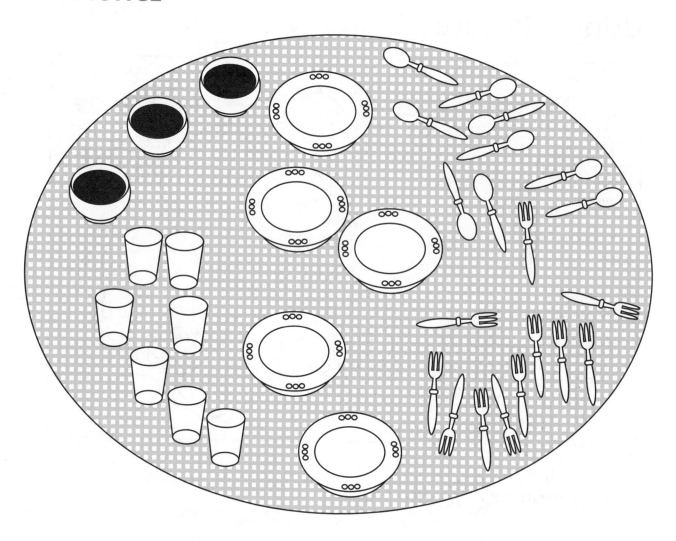

## Look at the picture.
## Write how many.

1. _____

2. _____

3. _____

4. _____

5. _____

# Using a Picture Graph

boat

car

How many  are there?

**A.** Ring the boat.

boat        car

**B.** Find the boat on the graph.

**C.** Count how many .

_____ 6

**Look at the graph.**
**Ring the answer.**

1. How many  are there?        3        4

2. Are there more  or  ?

• Comparing Numbers to 12

# PRACTICE

## Write how many.

1. _____

2. _____

3. _____

## Ring the answer.

4. Are there more  or  ?

5. Are there more  or  ?

6. Are there more  or ?

7. Ring the set that has the most.

# Underlining the Question

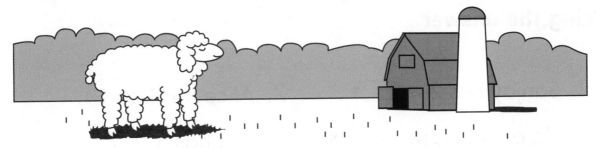

There are 3 big  on the farm.

There is I small .

How many  are on the farm?

**A.** Draw a line under the question.

How many  are on the farm?

- - - - - - - - - - - - - - - - - - - - - - - -

**B.** Ring the answer.

- farm

- 4

**C.** Read this new question.

Are there more than 3  on the farm?

- - - - - - - - - - - - - - - - - - - - - - - -

**D.** Ring the answer.

- 4

- yes

## Draw a line under the question.

There are 3  on the farm.  There is I .

How many more  are there?

●Numbers to I2

## PRACTICE

**Draw a line under the question.**
**Ring the answer.**

1. Sanjay has 2 .

   He gets 1 more .

   How many  does he have?

   • Sanjay

   • 3

2. Alice has 1 .

   She has 5 .

   How many more  does she have?

   • 4 more

   • no

3. Leon has 3 .

   Betsy has 5 .

   Does Betsy have more  than Leon?

   • yes

   • 2

4. June has 2 ◯.

   Gary has 3 ◯.

   Who has more ◯ ?

   • Gary

   • no

# Problem-Solving Practice

 fish  

 hamster  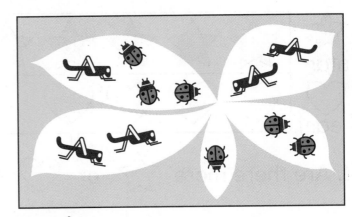

## Look at the graph.
## Ring the answer.

1. How many  are there?    2    3

2. Are there more  or  ?     

## Look at the picture.
## Write how many.

3. ____

4. ____

## Draw a line under the question.
## Ring the answer.

5. Lee sees 3  .    • 4     • Lee

    Kristen sees 1  .

    Who sees more  ?

# TEST-TAKING PRACTICE

## Ring the correct answer.

1. How many  are there?

- 4

- 5

---

star

heart

2. Are there more  or ♡ ?

- more ☆

- more ♡

---

3. Keith has 5 .

He has 3 🥕.

Does Keith have more 🍅

than 🥕?

- 5 🍅

- yes

© 1999 Metropolitan Teaching & Learning Co.

● Numbers to 12

**Name** _____

# Acting It Out

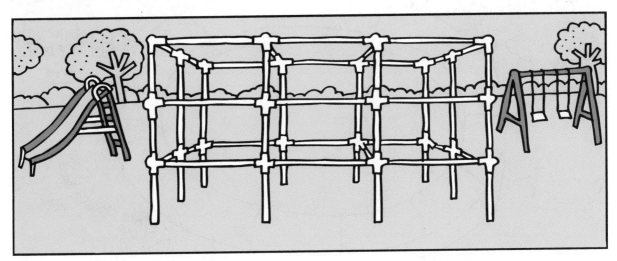

There are 3 ☺ on the ⊞.

Then I more ☺ comes.

How many ☺ are there now?

**A.** Use ●. Put 3 ● on the ⊞.

**B.** Add I more ● on the ⊞.

How many ☺ are there now? ____ ☺

**Use ●. Ring how many.**

There is I ☺ on the ⊞.  • ● ● ●

Then 2 more ☺ come.  • ● ● ● ● ●

● Addition Facts to 6

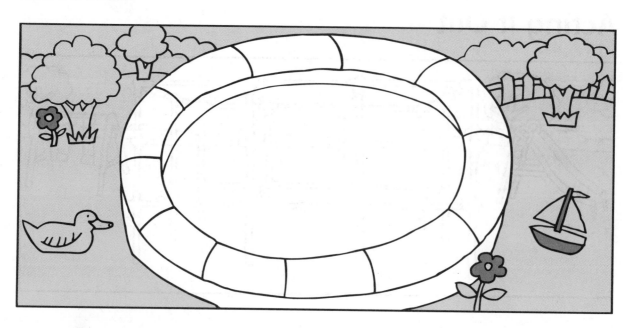

**Use ●. Solve.**

1. 2 😊 are in the 🛟.

Then 1 more 😊 comes.

How many 😊 are there

now? _____ 😊

2. 2 😊 are in the 🛟.

Then 2 more 😊 come.

How many 😊 are there

now? _____ 😊

3. 4 😊 are in the 🛟.

Then 2 more 😊 come.

How many 😊 are there

now? _____ 😊

4. 3 😊 are in the 🛟.

Then 2 more 😊 come.

How many 😊 are there

now? _____ 😊

# Using a Picture

How many 🎈 are there?

**A.** Look at the picture. Count.

How many 🎈 are by the ⊞ ? ____4____

How many 🎈 are by the 🪑 ? ____2____ 🎈

**B.** Add. Find how many 🎈 in all. ____6____ 🎈

## Use the picture. Write how many.

1. There are ____ 🕯 on the 🎂 .

   There are _____ 🕯 .

2. There are ____ 🎁 on the 🪑 .

   There is ____ 🎁 by the ⊞ .

● Addition Facts to 6

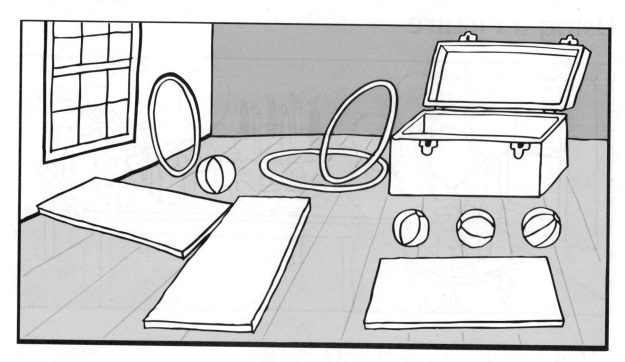

**Use the picture. Use ● to solve.**

1. There is _____ ⬭ by the ▦ .

   There are _____ ⬭ by the 🧰 .

   How many ⬭ are there? _____ ⬭

2. There are _____ ▱ by the ▦ .

   There is _____ ▱ by the 🧰 .

   How many ▱ are there? _____ ▱

3. There is _____ ◯ by the ▦ .

   There are _____ ◯ by the 🧰 .

   How many ◯ are there ? _____ ◯

# Writing a Number Sentence

**A.** Read the story.
   Start a number sentence.

   3 😊 play.

   Then 2 more 😊 come.    _3_ + _2_

   How many 😊 play now?

**B.** Add. Finish the sentence.    3 + 2 = _5_

## Read the story.
## Ring the number sentence that shows it.

1. 1 😊 plays on a swing.
   4 😊 play by the pool.
   • 1 + 3 = 4    • 1 + 4 = 5

2. 2 😊 play. Then 2 more 😊 come.
   • 2 + 2 = 4    • 2 + 1 = 3

• Addition Facts to 6

## PRACTICE
**Read the story. Use ⬤.**
**Write a number sentence.**

1. There are 3 🐕 playing.

   Then 1 more 🐕 comes.

   How many 🐕 are there?

   __3__ + __1__ = ____

2. 1 🐦 is in the 🥦.

   4 more 🐦 come.

   How many 🐦 are there?

   ____ + ____ = ____

3. 2 🐈 are by the 🪟.

   2 🐈 are by the 🪑.

   How many 🐈 are there?

   ____ + ____ = ____

4. There are 3 🙂 playing.

   2 🙂 sit in the 🌿.

   How many 🙂 are there?

   ____ + ____ = ____

5. 4 🙂 are in the 🏠.

   1 🙂 is in the 🚗.

   How many 🙂 are there?

   ____ + ____ = ____

6. Gia sees 2 🐟.

   3 more 🐟 come.

   How many 🐟 are there?

   ____ + ____ = ____

# Problem-Solving Practice

## Use the picture.

1. There are _____ 🦆 in the 🪺 .

   There are _____ 🦆 on the 🌿 .

   How many 🦆 are there? _____ 🦆

## Use ⚫.

2. Jan sees 3 ☺ in the park.

   Then 2 more ☺ come.

   How many ☺ does Jan see now? _____ ☺

## Write a number sentence.

3. Sue sees 1 🐿 near the 🌳 .

   She sees 3 🐿 by the 🪺 .

   How many 🐿 does Sue see in all?

   _____ + _____ = _____

● Addition Facts to 6

**Ring the correct answer.**

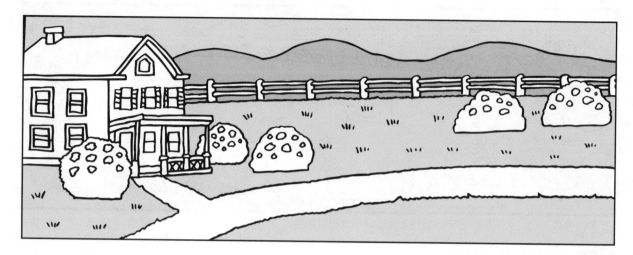

**Use the picture.**

1. There are _____ 🫓 by the 🏠 .
   • 3 🫓

   There are _____ 🫓 by the 🪵 .
   • 5 🫓

   How many 🫓 are there?

2. Elena sees 4 ☺ on the 🛝 .
   • 5 ☺

   She sees 2 ☺ on the 🏗 .
   • 6 ☺

   How many ☺ does she see?

3. Mike sees 3 🐕 in the yard.

   Then 1 more 🐕 comes.
   • 3 + 1 = 4

   How many 🐕 are there in all?
   • 3 + 2 = 5

• Addition Facts to 6

# Acting It Out

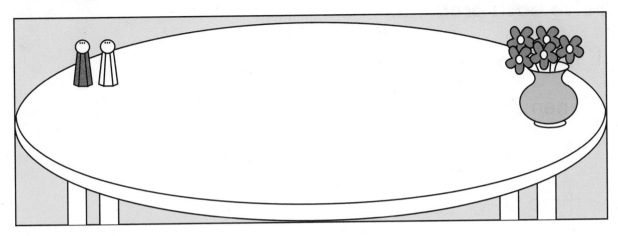

Sam has 5 🍎 . Then he eats 1 🍎 .

How many 🍎 does Sam have now?

**A.** Use ●. Put 5 ● on the 🛋.

**B.** Take away 1 ✋.

How many ● are left? _____ ●

How many 🍎 does Sam have now? _____ 🍎

**Use ●. Ring what to do with ●.**

1. Jim has 4 🍌 .

Then he eats 2 🍌 .

2. Jill has 5 🍐 .

Then she eats 3 🍐 .

● Subtraction Facts to 6

# PRACTICE

**Use** ●.
**Solve each problem.**

1. Ken saw 3 🐱.

   Then 2 🐱 ran away.

   How many 🐱 are

   there now? _____ 🐱

2. Kate saw 4 🐕.

   Then 1 🐕 ran away.

   How many 🐕 are there

   now? _____ 🐕

3. Bob saw 5 🐦.

   Then 4 🐦 left.

   How many 🐦 are there

   now? _____ 🐦

4. Bill saw 6 🐰.

   Then 4 🐰 left.

   How many 🐰 are there

   now? _____ 🐰

# Using a Picture

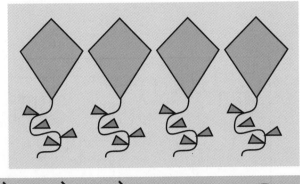
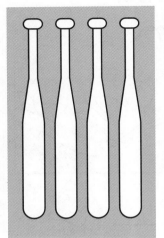
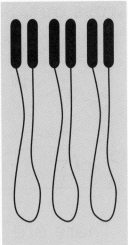
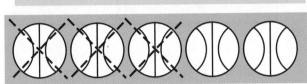

There are ___5___ .

Then Jack sells 3 .

How many  are left?

**A.** Cross out the 3  that Jack sells.

**B.** Write how many  now. ___2___

## Use the picture. Write how many.
## Cross out.

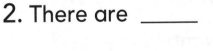

1. There are _____ .

   Then Jack sells 2 .

2. There are _____ .

   Then Jack sells 1 .

• **Subtraction Facts to 6**

# PRACTICE

## Use the picture. Write how many.
## Cross out. Solve.

1.

   There are _____  .

   Then I 🐦 leaves.

   How many are left?

   _____ 🐦

2.

   There are _____ 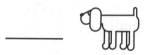 .

   Then 2 🐕 leave.

   How many are left?

   _____ 🐕

3.

   There are _____ 🐟 .

   Then 2 🐟 leave.

   How many are left?

   _____

4.

   There are _____ 🦢 .

   Then I 🦢 leaves.

   How many are left?

   _____ 🦢

# Writing a Number Sentence

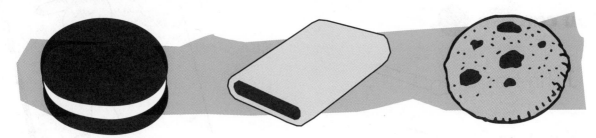

**A.** Read the story.

Start a number sentence.

Maria has 4 .  Ben has 2 .

How many more  does Maria have?

_4_ – _2_

**B.** Subtract.

Finish the sentence.  4 – 2 = _2_

**Read the story.**
**Ring the number sentence that shows it.**

1. John has 5 .

   He gives away 1 .

   How many  does

   John have left?

   • 5 – 1 = 4

   • 5 – 5 = 0

2. Kim has 3 .

   Dave has 2 .

   How many more

   does Kim have?

   • 3 – 2 = 1

   • 3 – 1 = 2

**Write a number sentence. Solve.
You can use ●.**

1. John has 5 🖌 .

   Kim has 2 🖌 .

   How many more 🖌 does John have?

   _____ – _____ = _____

2. Jee has 4 ✏ . Sadie has 1 ✏ .

   How many more ✏ does Jee have?

   _____ – _____ = _____

3. Maria has 6 🖍 . Then she gives 2 🖍 away.

   How many 🖍 does Maria have left?

   _____ – _____ = _____

4. Ben has 3 ✏ . Then he gives 2 ✏ away.

   How many ✏ does Ben have left?

   _____ – _____ = _____

Name _____

Name _____

---

Name _____

# Using Number Sense

Roberto sees 4 🦆 in the  .

Then 2 🦆 fly away.

How many 🦆 are left?

**A.** Act out the story. Use ●.

 Will I add more ● to 4?

Will I take away ● from 4?

**B.** Ring what you did.

- add more ●     • (take away ●)

**C.** Ring how many ● now.

- more than 4 ●     • (fewer than 4 ●)

**Read the story. Use ●.**
**Ring one answer.**

1. There are 6 🍎 on the 🌳.
   Then 5 🍎 fell off.
   How many 🍎 are on the 🌳 now?
   - more than 6 🍎
   - fewer than 6 🍎

2. There are 3 🐦 in the 🌳.
   Then 2 more 🐦 come.
   How many 🐦 are in the 🌳 now?
   - more than 3 🐦
   - fewer than 3 🐦

• Subtraction Facts to 6

Use  .

1. There are 6 🐿 by

   the .

   Then 3 🐿 go away.

   How many 🐿 are left?

   • more than 6 🐿

   • fewer than 6 🐿

2. Kisha sees 2 🐞 by

   the ❁.

   She sees 3 🐞 by the 🌳.

   How many 🐞 does

   Kisha see?

   • more than 2 🐞

   • fewer than 2 🐞

3. There are 3 🛒.

   Then Kisha takes 1 🛒.

   How many 🛒

   are left?

   • more than 3 🛒

   • fewer than 3 🛒

4. Jack has 2 🎈.

   Then Ann gives him 2 🎈.

   How many 🎈 does

   Jack have now?

   • more than 2 🎈

   • fewer than 2 🎈

# Problem-Solving Practice

**Solve.**
**Use the picture.**

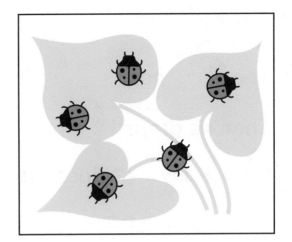

1. There are _____ 🐞 .

   Then 3 🐞 go away.

   How many 🐞 are left?

   _____ 🐞

2. There are 6 🦋.

   Then 2 🦋 fly away.

   How many 🦋 are there now?

   _____ 🦋

**Write a number sentence.**

3. Pete has 5 🎈 .

   Then Sam popped 2 of them.

   How many 🎈 does Pete have now?

   _____ − _____ = _____

**Ring the answer.**

4. Joyce has 6 🌼 .

   Then she gives 5 🌼 to Ben.

   How many 🌼 does Joyce have now?

   • more than 6 🌼　　　• fewer than 6 🌼

• Subtraction Facts to 6

# TEST-TAKING PRACTICE

**Ring the correct answer.**
**Use the picture.**

1. The  has ____ .

   Then he drops 1 .

   How many  does the  have left?

   - 4
   - 6

---

2. Lou has 4 .

   Then he gives Ed 1 .

   How many  does Lou have now?

   - 3
   - 5

---

3. Jill sees 3 .

   Then 2  run away.

   How many  are left?

   - $3 - 2 = 1$
   - $5 - 2 = 3$

---

4. Pat has 6 .

   Then he gives Jill 4 .

   How many  does Pat have now?

   - more than 6
   - fewer than 6

● Subtraction Facts to 6

# Using a Number Line

Joe has 2  in the .

Then he gets 3 more .

How many  are in the  now?

**A.** Use a number line.

How many  are there to start? ___2___

Put your finger 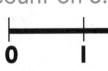 on number 2.

Count on 3.

```
        ⌢1⌢  ⌢2⌢  ⌢3⌢
  ──┼────┼────┼────┼────┼────┼───▶
    0    I    2    3    4    5    6
```

**B.** Write the number you end on. ___5___

**C.** Write how many  are in the  now.

___5___

**Ring the number line that shows the answer.**

There are 2 .

Then 4 more  come.

●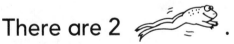
```
  ──┼──┼──┼──┼──┼──┼──▶
    0  I  2  3  4  5  6
```

●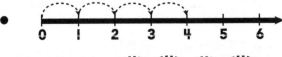
```
  ──┼──┼──┼──┼──┼──┼──▶
    0  I  2  3  4  5  6
```

© 1999 Metropolitan Teaching & Learning Co.

● Counting On

# PRACTICE

## Use the number line. Solve.

0  1  2  3  4  5  6

1. There are 3 . Then 1 more  comes.

How many  are there now? _____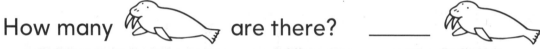

2. There are 2 . Then 4 more  come.

How many  are there? _____

3. Carol sees 1  jump. Paulo sees 4  jump.

How many  do they see in all? _____

4. Judy sees 2 . Then she sees 1 more .

How many does Judy see now? _____

Name _____

# Is the Answer a Word or a Number?

Bill has 4 🐰 . Sara has 2 🐰 .

Question 1. Who has more 🐰 ?

Question 2. How many 🐰 do they have in all?

**A.** Draw a line under question 1.

Who has more 🐰 ?
- - - - - - - - - - - - - - - - - -

**B.** Decide if the answer will be a word or a number.

Ring the answer.
- (a word)  • a number
- (Bill)  • 4 🐰

**C.** Draw a line under question 2.

How many 🐰 do they have in all?
- - - - - - - - - - - - - - - - - - - - - - - - - -

**D.** Decide if the answer will be a word or a number.

Ring the answer.
- a word  • (a number)
- Bill  • (6 🐰)

## Ring the kind of answer.

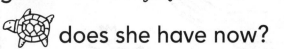

Joan has 1 🐢 . Then she gets 3 more 🐢 . How many 🐢 does she have now?

- word
- number

• Addition Facts to 6

**Decide what kind of answer. Solve.**

1. Lee sees 5  . Then 1 more  comes.

   How many  are there in all? _____

---

2. Sue sees 3  . Then 2 more  come.

   Are there more than 3  ? _____

---

3. There are 4  sitting. No more  come.

   How many  sit in all? _____

---

4. Tawana picks 3  . Ken picks 4 .

   Who has more ? _____

---

5. Lee sees 4 . Jim sees 4 .

   Does Lee see more  than Jim? _____

# Problem-Solving Practice

## Use the number line.

1. A bear has 3 🐟. Then the bear gets

   2 more 🐟. How many 🐟 does the bear have

   now? _____ 🐟

2. There are 4 🐦 in the tree.

   Then 2 more 🐦 come.

   How many 🐦 are in the

   tree now? _____ 🐦

## Decide what kind of answer. Solve.

3. Lee has 3 🍊. Kim has 2 🍊.

   Who has more 🍊? _____

4. Joe eats 2 🍌. Sue eats 2 🍌.

   How many 🍌 do Joe and Sue eat? _____

# TEST-TAKING PRACTICE

## Ring the correct answer.

## Use the number line.

1. There are 2 🦢.

   Then 3 more 🦢 come.        • 3 🦢

   How many 🦢 are there now?   • 5 🦢

---

**Solve.**

2. Pat sees 3 🦌. Lou sees 2 🦌.     • yes

   Do they see more than 4 🦌?     • 5 🦌

---

3. Sarina has 5 🐱.

   Rick has 2 🐱.                    • Sarina

   How many more 🐱 does           • 3 more 🐱

   Sarina have?

• Addition Strategies to 6

# Using a Number Line

🐻 has 4 🐟. He eats 2 🐟.

How many 🐟 does 🐻 have now?

**A.** Use a number line.

How many 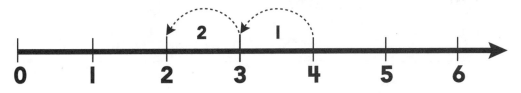 are there to start? __4__  🐟

Put your finger 👆 on number 4. Count back 2.

```
        2     1
    ⌒⌒⌒ ⌒⌒⌒
←———————————————————————————→
 0   1   2   3   4   5   6
```

**B.** Write the number you end on. __2__

Write how many 🐟 the 🐻 has now. __2__

## Ring the number line that shows the answer.

There are 3 🦌.

Then 2 🦌 walk away.

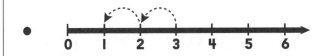

●
```
    ⌒⌒ ⌒⌒
←———————————————————→
 0  1  2  3  4  5  6
```

●
```
    ⌒⌒ ⌒⌒ ⌒⌒
←———————————————————→
 0  1  2  3  4  5  6
```

● Counting Back

# PRACTICE

## Use the number line. Solve.

1. Frank has 4 . Then he eats 1.

   How many are left? _____

---

2. Tanya has 3. Then she eats 2 .

   How many does she have left? _____

---

3. Joey makes 4. Sue eats 3 of them.

   How many are left for Joey? _____

---

4. Kay has 6. She gives 2 to Tanya.

   How many does Kay have left? _____

© 1999 Metropolitan Teaching & Learning Co.

**Name** _____

# Reading a Bar Graph

The children 😊 made a bar graph to show what bugs they saw in the park.

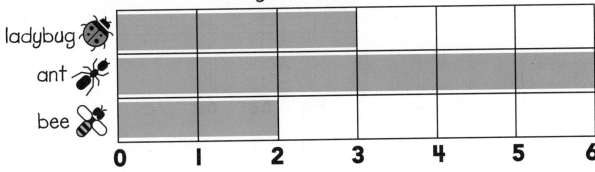

Bugs in the Park

How many more 🐜 than 🐝 did the 😊 see?

**A.** Use the bar graph to find how many.

How many bugs does each colored ☐ show? __1__

How many 🐜 did the 😊 see? __6__ 🐜

How many 🐝 did the 😊 see? __2__ 🐝

**B.** Subtract to find how many more 🐜 than 🐝 the 😊 saw.

__6__ – __2__ = __4__        __4__ more 🐜

## Use the graph.  Ring the answer.

1. How many 🐞 did the 😊 see?

   • 3 🐞    • 4 🐞

2. How many 🐝 and 🐞 did the 😊 see?

   • 4 bugs    • 5 bugs

• Comparative Subtraction

## Cost of Toys

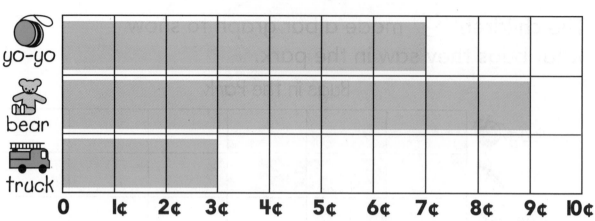

## Use the bar graph. Write the answer.

1. Which toy costs 7¢? _____

2. Which toy costs the most?

   _____

3. Which toy costs less than 5¢?

   _____

4. How much more does the  cost than the ?

   _____

5. How much more does the  cost than the ?

   _____

# Deciding Whether to Add or Subtract

There are 3 🐦 on the ▯▯ .

There are 2 🐦 in a 🌳 .

How many more 🐦 are on the ▯▯ ?

**A.** Draw a line under the question.

How many more 🐦 are on the ▯▯ ?

----------------------------------------

**B.** Decide whether to add or subtract.

THINK Would you add ● or take some away?

Ring one.        • add   • (subtract)

**C.** Write the number sentence. __3__ – __2__ = __1__

How many more 🐦 are on the ▯▯ ?        __1__ more

## Ring what to do to solve.

There are 2 🐦 on the 🌳 .

Then 2 more 🐦 come.

How many 🐦 are there in all?

• add

• subtract

• Addition and Subtraction Facts to 6

## PRACTICE
### Draw a line under the question. Solve.

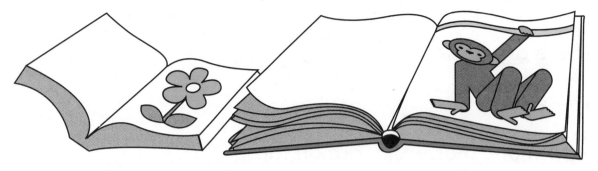

1. Maria has 3 big ▭. She has 3 small ▭.

   How many ▭ does she have in all? _____ ▭

2. Jeremy has 4 big ▭. He has 3 small ▭.

   How many fewer small ▭ does he have? _____ fewer

3. Helen has 4 big ▭. Kim gives Helen 2 small ▭.

   How many ▭ does Helen have in all? _____ ▭

4. Sam has 4 big ▭. He has 3 small ▭.

   Then Sam gets 2 more small ▭. How many

   small ▭ does he have? _____ small ▭

5. Raul has 4 big ▭. He has 3 small ▭.

   Then Raul gives away 1 small ▭. How many

   small ▭ does he have now? _____ small ▭

# Problem-Solving Practice

## Solve. Use the number line.

1. Sid has 6 . He gives his sister 2 .

   How many  does he have now?    _____

## Draw a line under the question.

2. Jim has 4 🐱.  He has 2 🐶. How many

   more 🐱 than 🐶 does he have? _____ more 🐱

## Use the graph.

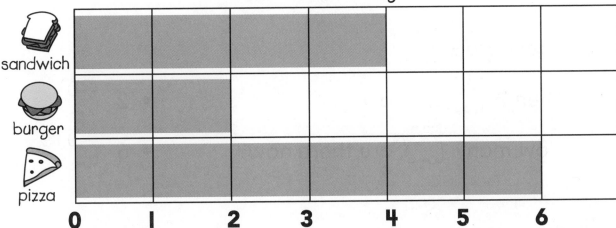

Food for Lunch Today

3. How many more  were chosen than 🍔 ?

   _____ more

© 1999 Metropolitan Teaching & Learning Co.

## Ring the correct answer.
## Use the bar graph.

Coins in Jim's Pocket

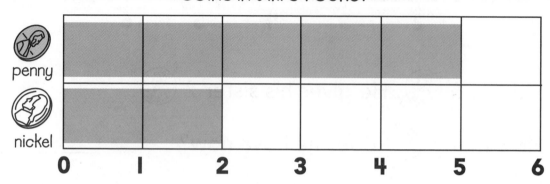

1. How many more  than  does Jim have?

   • 3 more

   • 5 more

## Use the number line.

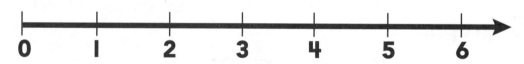

2. There are 4  .

   Then 2  run away.

   How many  are there now?

   • 2

   • 6

3. Sid had 2  . Then he got

   3  from Sam. How many

    does Sid have now?

   • 1

   • 5

• Subtraction Strategies to 6

# Reading a Table

## Balloons for Clowns

| clowns | Silly  | Happy  | Giggles  |
|---|---|---|---|
|  balloons | 35 | 61 | 49 |

How many  does  have?

**A.** Look at the table. Ring one.
The top row shows • (clowns) • balloons
The bottom row shows • clowns • (balloons)

**B.** Look at the names and numbers in the table.

How many  does  have? __35__

Who has 49  ? __Giggles__

**Use the table. Ring the answer.**

1. How many  does

    have?

   • 49

   • 61

2. Who has more  ?

   • 

   • 

• Comparing Numbers to 99

## Number of Stickers

| name | Jason | Lara | Rosa | Rob |
|---|---|---|---|---|
| 🎪 stickers | 85 | 80 | 59 | 72 |

## Use the table. Write the answer.

1. How many stickers does Lara have? _____

2. Who has 72 stickers? _____

3. Does Rosa have more stickers than Lara?_____

4. Who has fewer stickers than Rob? _____

5. Who has the most stickers? _____

6. Who has more stickers than Rob?_____

   and _____

# Making a Table

## Pails for Shells

| pails | 1 | 2 | 3 | 4 | 5 | 6 |
|---|---|---|---|---|---|---|
| shells | 10 | 20 | 30 | 40 | 50 | 60 |

Pat puts 10 🐚 in a 🪣. How many 🐚 can she put into 6 🪣?

**A.** Make a table to find out.

Write the numbers of 🪣 in the first row.

How many more 🪣 are in each box

as you go across? ____1____ more 🪣

**B.** Write the numbers of 🐚 in the bottom row.

What number do you count by as you go across? __10__

**C.** Write how many 🐚 Pat can put into 6 🪣. __60__

## Use the table. Ring the answer.

1. How many 🐚 are

   in 3 🪣?

   • 3 🐚    • 30 🐚

2. How many 🪣 does

   Pat need for 20 🐚?

   • 20 🪣    • 2 🪣

• Place Value to 100

## PRACTICE

Mark puts 4 🌼 in a 🏺.

### Vases for Flowers

| 🏺 vases | 1 | 2 | 3 | 4 | _____ |
|---|---|---|---|---|---|
| 🌼 flowers | 4 | 8 | _____ | _____ | _____ |

## Complete the table. Write the answer.

1. How many 🌼 are in 5 🏺?

   _____

2. How many 🌼 can Mark put in 3 🏺?

   _____

3. How many 🏺 does Mark need for 16 🌼?

   _____

4. Do 3 🏺 have more than 20 🌼?

   _____

5. Do 3 🏺 have fewer than 15 🌼?

   _____

# Is the Answer a Word or a Number?

Pete 19     Jeff 36     Kay 25

Did Pete pick more  than Kay?

**A.** Find how many  each has.

Pete ___19___

Kay ___25___

**B.** Compare. Write the number that is more. ___25___

**C.** Read the question. Decide what kind of answer.

Did Pete pick more  than Kay ?

**THINK** Will the answer be a number or a word?

Ring one.     • 6 more      •(no)

## Ring to show if the answer is a word or a number.

1. Does Pete have fewer  than Jeff?

   • word     • number

2. How many more  does Jeff have than Kay?

   • word     • number

• Comparing Numbers to 99

## Decide if the answer is a word or a number. Then solve.

1. Does Pete have more 🍐 than Ben? _____

2. Who has more 🍐 than Anu? _____

3. How many 🍐 does Anu have?_____ .

4. Who has fewer 🍐 than Pete? _____

5. How many 🍐 does the child with the most have?

_____

# Problem-Solving Practice

## Ring the answer.

### Baskets for Eggs

| baskets | 1 | 2 | 3 | _____ |
|---|---|---|---|---|
| eggs | 6 | 12 | 18 | _____ |

## Complete the table.

1. How many ◯ fit in 4 🧺 ?

   • 20 ◯        • 24 ◯

2. Ann wants 18 ◯ . How many 🧺
   will she get?

   • 2 🧺        • 3 🧺

3. Margaret has 42 .
   Her friend Nick has 38 🍓.
   Who has more 🍓 ?

   • 4 more         • Margaret

# TEST-TAKING PRACTICE

## Ring the correct answer.

43 shells
Leah

29 shells
Angie

61 shells
Joe

## Use the picture.

1. Does Leah have more 🐚 than Angie?

2. Who has more 🐚 than Leah?

- 43 🐚
- yes
- 61 🐚
- Joe

## Complete the table.

### Pails of Clams

| pails | 1 | 2 | 3 | 4 | 5 | _____ |
|-------|---|---|---|---|---|-------|
| clams | 5 | _____ | 15 | 20 | _____ | _____ |

3. How many 🐚 are in 4 pails?

- 20 🐚
- 25 🐚

4. How many 🪣 would 30 🐚 fill?

- 5 🪣
- 6 🪣

● Place Value to 100

# Reading a Schedule

| SHOW | | TIME |
|---|---|---|
| Clown Show | | 12:00–1:00 |
| Acrobat Show | | 1:00–2:00 |
| Dance Show | | 2:00–2:30 |

Meg met Jo at the end of the Dance Show.
What time was it?

**A.** Use the schedule. Find the Dance Show.

What time does that show start? _____ 2:00

What time does that show end? _____ 2:30

**B.** Use the time found to answer the question.

What time did Meg meet Jo? _____ 2:30

## Use the schedule. Ring the show that starts at the time on the clock.

1.  • Acrobat Show    • Clown Show

2.  • Dance Show    • Acrobat Show

• Time to Hour and Half-Hour

# PRACTICE

## Sports Day Schedule

| | | |
|---|---|---|
| 9:00 | relay race | |
| 10:00 | sack race | |
| 10:30 | jump rope | |
| 11:30 | hop scotch | |

Read the schedule. Ring the activity that starts at the time on the clock.

1. • hop scotch   • sack race   • jump rope

2. • hop scotch   • jump rope   • relay race

3. • relay race   • sack race   • hop scotch

4. • sack race   • hop scotch   • jump rope

# Reading a Calendar

| | | | SEPTEMBER | | | |
|---|---|---|---|---|---|---|
| Sunday | Monday | Tuesday | Wednesday | Thursday | Friday | Saturday |
| | | | 1 | 2 | 3 | 4 |
| 5 | 6 | 7 | 8 | 9 | 10 | 11 |
| 12 | 13 | 14 | 15 | 16 | 17 | 18 |
| 19 | 20 | 21 | 22 | 23 | 24 | 25 |
| 26 | 27 | 28 | 29 | 30 | | |

The date that Jay swims is September 22.
What day of the week is that?

**A.** Look at the top of the calendar.
Read the days of the week.

**B.** Find the number 22 on the calendar.
What day of the week is September 22 under?

Wednesday

**Use the calendar. Ring the answer.**

1. What day of the week is September 9?
   - Friday
   - Thursday

2. Is September 16 a day of the week or a date?
   - a day of the week
   - a date

# PRACTICE

| | | FEBRUARY | | | | |
|---|---|---|---|---|---|---|
| Sunday | Monday | Tuesday | Wednesday | Thursday | Friday | Saturday |
| | | | | | | 1 |
| 2 | 3 | 4 | 5 | 6 | 7 | 8 |
| 9 | 10 | 11 | 12 | 13 | 14 | 15 |
| 16 | 17 | 18 | 19 | 20 | 21 | 22 |
| 23 | 24 | 25 | 26 | 27 | 28 | |

## Use the calendar. Write the answer.

1. What day of the week comes after Tuesday?

_____

2. What day of the week is February 14?

_____

3. What date is the first Monday of February?

_____

4. How many Wednesdays does February have?

_____ Wednesdays

# Using Coins

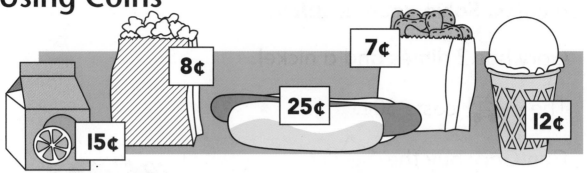

Bob has 4 nickels. Can he buy a  ?

**A.** Use coins to find how much Bob has.

Put 4 nickels down.

THINK

What do you count by?    5¢   10¢   15¢   20¢

**B.** Compare amounts.

How much does a  cost?    25¢

Can Bob buy a 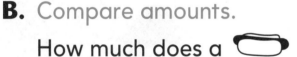 ? Ring one.    • yes    • (no)

## Use the picture. Use coins. Ring the answer.

1. Jill has 1 dime and 2 nickels. Can she buy  ?

   • yes        • no

2. Lee has 2 pennies and a nickel. Can she buy a  ?

   • yes        • no

3. Al has 9 pennies. Can he buy a  ?

   • yes        • no

4. Roy has 1 dime. Can he buy an  ?

   • yes        • no

# PRACTICE

## Use coins. Solve each problem.

1. Gary has 2 dimes and a nickel.

   The  costs 30¢.

   Can Gary buy the ? _____

---

2. Joel wants a 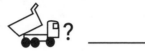.

   It costs 46¢. He has I quarter,

   2 dimes, and 3 pennies.

   Can he buy it? _____

---

3. Debbie sees a .

   She has 3 dimes and 2 pennies.

   Can she buy the ⊘ for 30¢? _____

---

4. Karen wants a .

   It costs 41¢.

   Can she buy it with 6 nickels? _____

# Problem-Solving Practice

**Write the answer.**
**Use the schedule.**

| CLASS | TIME |
|---|---|
| Science | 9:00 – 10:30 |
| Math | 10:30 – 12:00 |
| Gym | 12:00 – 1:30 |

1. What time does Math start?

_____

2. What time does Science end?

_____

| ☂ APRIL ☂ | | | | | | |
|---|---|---|---|---|---|---|
| Sunday | Monday | Tuesday | Wednesday | Thursday | Friday | Saturday |
| | 1 | 2 | 3 | 4 | 5 | 6 |
| 7 | 8 | 9 | 10 | 11 | 12 | 13 |
| 14 | 15 | 16 | 17 | 18 | 19 | 20 |
| 21 | 22 | 23 | 24 | 25 | 26 | 27 |
| 28 | 29 | 30 | | | | |

**Use the calendar.**

3. What is the date of the first Friday of April?

April _____

**Use coins.**

4. Sue has 5 dimes. Can she buy a  for 50¢?

_____

# TEST-TAKING PRACTICE

## Ring the correct answer.

1. Sam has 6 nickels.
   Can he buy a drink for 25¢?

   - yes
   - no

| GAME | TIME |
|------|------|
| Tag | 2:30 – 3:30 |
| Relay | 3:30 – 4:30 |
| Ball | 4:30 – 6:00 |

2. Which game ends at 4:30?

   - relay
   - ball

| ❄ JANUARY ❄ | | | | | | |
|---|---|---|---|---|---|---|
| Sunday | Monday | Tuesday | Wednesday | Thursday | Friday | Saturday |
| | | 1 | 2 | 3 | 4 | 5 |
| 6 | 7 | 8 | 9 | 10 | 11 | 12 |
| 13 | 14 | 15 | 16 | 17 | 18 | 19 |
| 20 | 21 | 22 | 23 | 24 | 25 | 26 |
| 27 | 28 | 29 | 30 | 31 | | |

3. What day of the week
   is January 4?

   - Thursday
   - Friday

4. What date is the last
   Wednesday in January?

   - January 30
   - January 31

**Name** _____

# Drawing a Picture

There are 5 🔘 on Sue's 👕. Sam has 4 🔘 on his 👕. How many 🔘 do Sam and Sue have?

**A.** Draw a picture to show the problem.

Draw Sue's 5 🔘.

Draw Sam's 4 🔘.

**B.** Read the question again.

**THINK** Do you add or subtract?

How many 🔘 do Sam and Sue have?  _____

## Ring the picture that shows the problem.

1. Sue has 3 🔘 on her 🦺. Mai has 5 🔘 on hers. How many more 🔘 does Mai have?

   • ○○○ / ○○○○○

   • ○○○ + ○○○○○

2. Malik has 7 🔘 on his 🧥. Then he loses 2 🔘. How many 🔘 does Malik have now?

   • ✗✗○○○○○

   • ○○ + ○○○○○○○

● Choosing the Operation

## Practice

### Draw a picture that shows the problem. Solve.

1. Jan has 2 🎈. Then she gets 6 more 🎈. How many 🎈 does she have now?

   _____ 🎈

2. Jane has 7 🎈. She has 3 more 🎈 than Gina. How many 🎈 does Gina have?

   _____ 🎈

3. Lee gives Jan 4 of her 🎈. Now Lee has 3 🎈. How many 🎈 did Lee have before?

   _____ 🎈

4. Ben has 9 🎈. Then I 🎈 pops and 2 🎈 fly away. How many 🎈 does Ben have now?

   _____ 🎈

# Using a Number Line

The 🐰 eats 7 🥕 in the garden. Then the 🐰 eats

3 more 🥕. How many 🥕 does she eat in all?

**A.** Use a number line to help.

Put your 👉 on the number of 🥕 the 🐰 eats first.

What number is that? ___7___

**B.** Decide what to do. Ring one.

- ⟨count on 3⟩    • count back 3

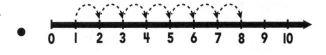

How many 🥕 does she eat in all? ___10___ 🥕

## Ring the number line that shows the problem.

A 🐿 has 7 🌰. Then

he eats 6 🌰. How many

🌰 does he have left?

•

## Practice

**Use the number line.**
**Ring <u>count on</u> or <u>count back</u>. Solve.**

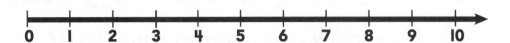

1. Jake has 6 . Then he gives Noah 2 .

   How many  does Jake have now?

   • count on        • count back      _____

2. Noah has 6 . Then he gets 3 more .

   How many  does he have now?

   • count on        • count back      _____

3. Jake has 4 . He puts them with May's .

   May has 3 . How many  do they have in all?

   • count on        • count back      _____

4. Matt has 5 . Then he gives 2  to Kay.

   How many  does Matt have now?

   • count on        • count back      _____

# Acting It Out

Ken had 7 ◯. Then he picked _____ more ◯.

Now he has 10 ◯. How many more ◯ did he pick?

**A.** Use cubes to solve.

How many ◯ did Ken have? __7__ ◯

Put 7 cubes together.

**B.** How many ◯ does Ken have in all? __10__ ◯

Put 10 cubes together.

**C.** Find how many more cubes will make both rows

the same. __3__ more

How many more ◯ did Ken pick? __3__ more

## Draw more cubes to find the missing number.

Ken made 3 egg 🥪. He made

_____ jam 🥪. He has 8 🥪 in all.

How many jam 🥪 did he make?

• Missing Addends

## Practice

## Use cubes to show the amount. Solve.

1. Kate packed 7 ☐. Then she packed _____ more. She has 9 ☐ in all. How many more ☐ did she pack? _____ more ☐

---

2. Kate needs 10 ☐ of juice in all. She made 2 ☐ and then she made _____ more ☐. How many more ☐ did she make? _____ more ☐

---

3. Kate used 5 ◯ to make juice. Then she put in _____ more. In all she used 9 ◯. How many more ◯ did she put in? _____ more ◯

---

4. Each ☐ had a ◯. Kate had 3 ◯. Then she bought _____ more ◯. She put 9 ◯ in the ☐ in all. How many more ◯ did she buy? _____ more ◯

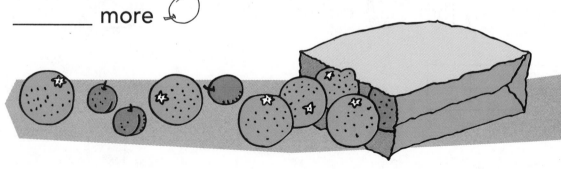

# Problem-Solving Practice

**Solve each problem.**
**Use the number line.**

1. Kay has 8 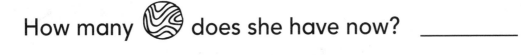. Then she gives Ed 5 . How many does she have now? _____

2. Lee has 5 . Then he finds 3 more . How many does he have now? _____

**Draw a picture.**

3. Ling has 6 . Then he gets 4 more . How many does he have now? _____

**Use cubes.**

4. Ben saw 4 . Then _____ more joined them. Now there are 9 . How many joined the first 4 ? _____

# TEST-TAKING PRACTICE

## Ring the correct answer.

1. Meg had 4 🥧 . Then she made _____   • 5 🥧

   more 🥧 . Now she has 9 🥧 in all.   • 6 🥧

   How many 🥧 did she make?

---

2. Rick has 7 🐟 .   • 2 🐟

   Jenny has 2 more 🐟 than Rick.   • 9 🐟

   How many 🐟 does Jenny have?

---

3. Bill gets 6 🧁 . Then he eats 1 🧁 .   • 5 🧁

   How many 🧁 does he have now?   • 7 🧁

---

4. Joel finds 5 🦀 . He puts them in a pail.   • 5 🦀

   Judy has 3 🦀 . She puts her 🦀 in   • 8 🦀

   the pail. How many 🦀 are in the pail?

---

5. Ben uses 6 🍋 to make a pie.   • 4 🍋

   Then he puts 2 more 🍋 into the pie.   • 8 🍋

   How many 🍋 does he use in all?

• Addition and Subtraction Facts to 10

# Looking for a Pattern

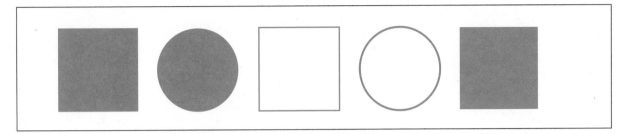

## What comes next in the pattern?

**A.** Look at the shapes in the pattern.
Name each shape as you point to it.
Write the next shape.
square  circle  square  circle  square  <u>circle</u>

**B.** Look at the colors in the pattern.
Name each color as you point to it.
Write the next color.
red  red  white  white  red  <u>red</u>

**C.** Write the color and shape of what comes next
in the pattern.  <u>red</u>        <u>circle</u>

## Look at the pattern.
## Ring the shape that comes next.

1. ▢▢▢●▢▢▢●

   • ▢

   • ●

2. ●■▢■●○▢○●■

   • ●

   • ■

# PRACTICE

## Look for the pattern. Draw the next shape.

1.

2.

3.

4.

5.

6.

# Drawing a Picture

May makes 4 ⬭. She puts a ☆ on 1 ⬭. What part of May's ⬭ have a ☆?

**A.** Draw 4 ⬭. Draw a ☆ on 1 ⬭.

⬭ ⬭ ⬭ ⬭

How many ⬭ have a ☆?  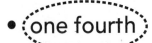 ___1___

How many ⬭ are there in all?  ___4___

**B.** Ring the fraction that shows what part of the ⬭ have ☆.

• one half     • one third     • **one fourth**

## Ring the picture that shows the part.

1. Lou puts a ☆ on one third of his 3 ⬭.

2. Jill puts a ♡ on one half of her 2 ⬭.

• Fractions of a Set

## PRACTICE

**Draw a picture to show the part.**
**Ring the correct fraction.**

1.  Jed has 3 ⬬. 1 ⬬ is blue. What part of Jed's ⬬ are blue?

    • one third   • one half

2.  Cary has 4 🐱. 1 🐱 is white. What part of Cary's 🐱 are white?

    • one third   • one fourth

3.  Kit has 2 📖. 1 📖 is big. What part of Kit's 📖 are big?

    • one half   • one third

4.  Ben has 3 🪴. 1 🪴 is small. What part of Ben's 🪴 are small?

    • one half   • one third

# Problem-Solving Practice

**Look for a pattern.**
**Draw the next shape.**

1.

2.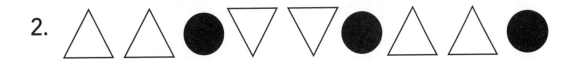

**Ring the picture that shows the part.**

3. There is a ☆ on one third of the 3 ⬭.

   • [star cookie] [cookie]

   • [cookie] [star cookie] [cookie]

4. Maria's mom bakes 4 🍩. She puts a 🌸 on
   1 🍩. What part of the 🍩 have a 🌸?

   • one third

   • one fourth

• Geometry and Fractions

**Ring the correct answer.**
**Choose the one that shows the next shape.**

1.

   -

   - ○

2.

   - ■

   - ●

3. ● ♡ ● ● ♡ ● ● ● ♡ ● ♡

   - ♡

   - ●

**Ring the picture that shows the part.**

4. Tom drew a 🌼 on one third of his 3 papers.

   -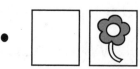

   -

5. Tina has 4 papers. She draws a ♥ on 1 of her papers. What part of Tina's papers have a ♥?

   - one fourth

   - one half

● Geometry and Fractions

# Drawing a Picture

Jake is the fourth 😊 in line at the fair. There are

6 😊 behind him. How many 😊 are in the line?

**A.** Draw circles to show each 😊. First draw 4.

Put a J in the fourth circle to show Jake.

◯ ◯ ◯ Ⓙ

**B.** Draw a circle for each 😊 behind Jake.

◯ ◯ ◯ Ⓙ ◯ ◯ ◯ ◯ ◯ ◯

**C.** Count how many circles in all. __10 circles__

How many 😊 are in line? ___10___ 😊

## Ring the picture that shows the problem.

There are 7 😊 in line.
Davey is in the middle of the
line. How many 😊 are in
front of Davey?

• ◯ ◯ ◯ Ⓓ ◯ ◯ ◯

• ◯ Ⓓ ◯ ◯ ◯ ◯ ◯

• Addition and Subtraction Facts to 18

## PRACTICE

### Draw to show the problem. Solve.

1. Pat threw 5  at the Duck Game. She has 8 ◯ left. How many ◯ did she start with?

_____ ◯

2. There are 2 rows of 🪑 in the tent. There are 7 🪑 in each row. How many 🪑 are there in all?

_____ 🪑

3. Greg is sixth in line. The same number of  are behind him and in front of him. How many are in line?

_____ ☺

4. Kelly went on 14 rides. She went on 9 rides in the afternoon. How many rides did she go on in the morning?

_____ rides

**Name** _____

# Acting It Out

Meg makes 4 gift bags for her friends at her party. She has 16 . How many  can she put in each bag?

**A.** Act it out. First draw 4 circles.

◯ ◯ ◯ ◯

**B.** Put 16 ● into the circles, one at a time.

How many ● are in each circle?  ____ 4 ●

How many  can Meg put in each bag?  ____ 4

## Ring what to do to act out the problem.

Meg has 15 treats. Then she gives 2 each to her 4 friends. How many are left?

• Place 4 ● in 2 circles.

• Place 2 ● each in 4 circles. Count how many are left.

• Addition and Subtraction Facts to 18

## PRACTICE

**Use counters to act out the problem. Solve.**

1. Meg gives each of her 4 friends a plate. Each plate has 3 . How many  do all her friends get?

   _____

2. Meg has 13 🎈. She gives 3 🎈 to Sam and 4 🎈 to Max. She gives all the other 🎈 to Sarah. How many 🎈 does Sarah get?

   _____

3. Sarah gives Meg a bag of 15 ⚪. Meg makes 2 necklaces. She puts 6 ⚪ on each necklace. How many ⚪ does she have left?

   _____

4. Sam gives Meg a bag of 12 whistles. Meg gives 3 to Sarah and 5 to Max. How many whistles does she give away?

   _____

# Underlining Needed Information

Bill has 17 🚗. Then he gives 9 🚗 to Frank.

Bill and Frank have been friends for 3 years.

How many 🚗 does Bill have now?

**A.** Draw a line under the information you need to solve the problem.

Bill has 17 🚗. Then he gives 9 🚗 to Frank.
-----------------------------------------------

Bill and Frank have been friends for 3 years.

How many 🚗 does Bill have now?

**B.** Use the information. Solve.

How many 🚗 does Bill have now? _____

**Ring the problem that has lines under the information you need.**

- Cary has 6 🚗.
  Then she gets 5 🚗
  from Jane. Matt gives
  Jane 3 🚗.
  How many 🚗 does
  Cary have now?

- Cary has 6 🚗.
  Then she gets 5 🚗
  from Jane. Matt gives
  Jane 3 🚗.
  How many 🚗 does
  Cary have now?

## PRACTICE

**Draw a line under the information you need. Solve.**

1. Karen puts 8 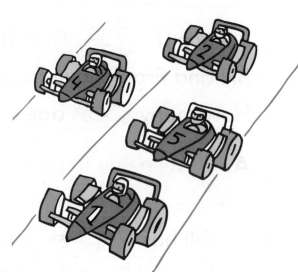 on the track. Joan puts 6 on the track. Joan has 8 more in her box. How many are on the track?

   _____

2. Joan has 15 red and blue . She has 7 blue . Karen has 6 red . How many of Joan's are red?

   _____

3. Mark has 2 yellow . He also has 3 red and 7 blue . Joan has 7 blue , too. How many blue do Mark and Joan have?

   _____ blue

4. Karen has 2 red . Mark has 15 . Mark gives 6 red to Karen. Now Karen has 8 red . How many does Mark have now?

   _____

# Problem-Solving Practice

## Solve each problem.

**Draw a picture.**

1. There are 6 😊 in line. Siva has 2 😊 behind her. How many 😊 are in front of her? _____ 😊

2. Gary eats 4 🍪. Jan eats 7 🍪. How many more 🍪 does Jan eat? _____ more 🍪

**Use counters.**

3. Ned gives 5 ⭐ to each of his 3 friends. How many ⭐ does he give away in all? _____ ⭐

**Draw a line under the information you need. Then solve.**

4. Hans gives Lisa 9 red 🔘 and 5 blue 🔘. He gives Ricky 4 red 🔘. How many red 🔘 does Hans give? _____ red 🔘

• Addition and Subtraction Facts to 18

# TEST-TAKING PRACTICE

## Ring the correct answer.

1. Kali has 13 🎈 . She gives 4 🎈 to Eric. She gives 3 🎈 to Ling. How many 🎈 does she have now?

   • 5 🎈

   • 6 🎈

2. Kate puts 3 🎈 in her bag. She puts 4 🎈 on the table. Hank puts 5 🎈 on the table. How many 🎈 are on the table?

   • 9 🎈

   • 12 🎈

3. Alice is fifth in line. There are 11 🙂 behind her. How many 🙂 are in line?

   • 11 🙂

   • 16 🙂

4. Jill has 17 🃏 . She gives 9 to Mike. Mike gives 5 🃏 to Tom. How many 🃏 does Jill have now?

   • 4 🃏

   • 8 🃏

© 1999 Metropolitan Teaching & Learning Co.

● Addition and Subtraction Facts to 18

**Name** _____

# Drawing a Picture

Dan has 2 quarts of apple juice. He needs 3 pints of apple juice. Does he have enough?

**A.** Draw to show how much Dan has.

Dan has 2 quarts. [Q] [Q]

**B.** Show the quarts as pints.

THINK How many pints are in a quart?

I quart is __2__ pints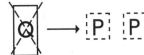

2 quarts are __4__ pints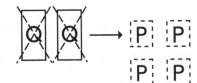

**C.** Read the question again.

Decide if Dan has enough. • (yes) • no

---

## Ring the picture that shows the problem.

Dan has 2 pints of apple juice. He needs a quart. Does he have enough?

• [P] [P] ⟶ [Q]

• [P] [P] ⟶ [Q] [Q]

• Capacity

**Draw to show the amount.**
**Ring yes or no.**

1. Joy has 2 quarts of grape juice. She needs 4 pints. Does she have enough?

   • yes          • no

2. Kim has 6 pints of milk. He needs 2 quarts. Does he have enough?

   • yes          • no

3. Gail has 1 quart of water. She needs 3 pints. Does she have enough?

   • yes          • no

4. Don has 5 pints of orange juice. He needs 3 quarts. Does he have enough?

   • yes          • no

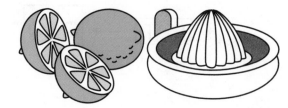

# Deciding Which Unit to Use

Ned's  is 6 inches tall. Keesha's  is 11 inches tall. How much taller is Keesha's ?

**A.** Write a subtraction sentence.

$$\underline{11} - \underline{6} = \underline{5}$$

**B.** Read the question again. Remember to write the unit of measurement after the number.

How much taller is Keesha's 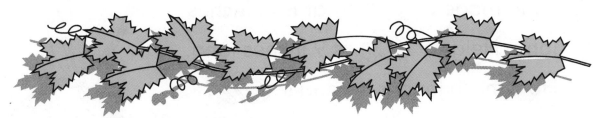?

5 <u>inches</u>

## Ring the correct answer.

1. Eva used 7 cups of water for her 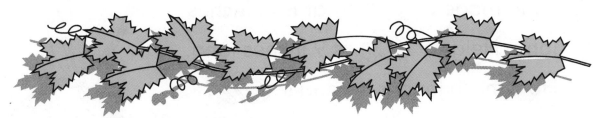. Then she used 2 more cups of water. How many cups did Eva use in all?

   • 9 cups

   • 9 pints

2. Jed's was 12 inches long. Then it grew 4 more inches. How long is Jed's now?

   • 16 feet

   • 16 inches

• Measurement

**Solve. Write the unit of measurement.**

1. Jeri has 3 cups of milk. Siva has 2 cups of milk. How much milk do they have together?

   _____

2. Taro adds 9 inches to his 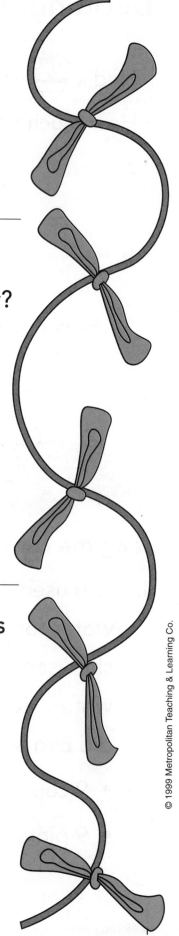 .
   It was 7 inches long. How long is it now?

   _____

3. Lena made a that is 14 inches long. Helga's is 9 inches long. How much longer is Lena's ?

   _____

4. Joe used 3 pints of juice. He had 7 pints to start with. How many pints of juice are left?

   _____

**Name** _____

# Not Enough Information

Lisa's ⬭ is 4 feet long. Kim's ⬭ is longer than Lisa's. How much longer is Kim's ⬭?

**A.** Think about what the problem tells.

Ring <u>yes</u> or <u>no</u>.

Do you know how long Lisa's ⬭ is?

• (yes)          • no

Do you know how long Kim's ⬭ is?

• yes          • (no)

**B.** Decide whether you know enough to solve the problem.     • yes          • (no)

**Solve the problem if you can.**
**If not, ring <u>need more information</u>.**

1. Lisa is 6 years old. Kim jumps more. She is 1 year older. How old is Kim?

   • _____

   • need more information

2. Kim jumps rope faster than Lisa. Kim is 2 inches taller. How tall is Lisa?

   • _____

   • need more information

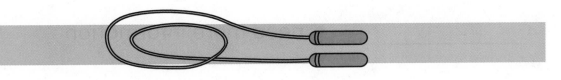

• Linear Measurement

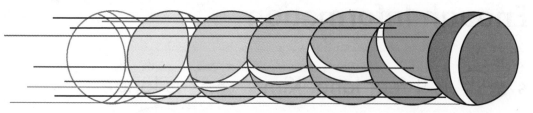

## Solve the problem if you can.
## If not, ring need more information.

1. Andy throws the ◖ 13 feet. The ◖ goes 9 feet when Ben throws it. How much farther does Andy throw the ◖?

   _____  • need more information

2. Mary can jump 3 feet. Andy can jump 1 foot more. Who is older?

   _____  • need more information

3. Ben's 🪱 is 10 inches long. Andy's 🪱 is just as long. Ben adds 3 inches to his . Whose 🪱 is longer?

   _____  • need more information

4. Marita throws a ◖ 11 feet. Kathy is 2 years older than Marita. Kathy throws the ◖ farther. How much farther does Kathy's ◖ go?

   _____  • need more information

# Problem-Solving Practice

**Draw a picture. Solve.**

1. Jed has 2 quarts of milk. He needs 3 pints. Does he have enough?

   _____

2. Kelly mixes 3 pints of apple juice with 1 quart of grape juice. How many pints does she make in all?

   _____ pints

**Ring the answer.**

3. Kai makes a [chain] that is 7 inches long. Sara makes a [chain] that is 9 inches long. How long are both [chain] together?

   • 16 inches          • 2 feet

4. Lisa is 6 years old. Vicki is 7. Lisa is 4 feet tall. How much taller is Vicki?

   • 1 foot          • not enough information

# TEST-TAKING PRACTICE

## Ring the correct answer.

1.  Abram needs 5 pints of juice. He buys 2 quarts. Does he have enough?

    - yes
    - no

---

2.  Jan has 5 cups of milk. He needs 2 pints to make pudding. Does he have enough milk?

    - yes
    - no

---

3.  Juan makes a ✐ that is 4 inches long. He adds 5 more inches to his ✐. How long is it now ?

    - 9 inches
    - 9 feet

---

4.  Paul uses 8 inches of ✐. Alice uses 3 inches. How many inches of ✐ do they use in all?

    - 11 inches
    - not enough information

- Measurement

Name _____

# Using Dimes and Pennies

Luis has 23 blue  and 35 red .

How many  does he have in all?

**A.** Use pennies and dimes to help you add.

Let 1 penny stand for 1 .

Let 1 dime stand for 10 .

How many blue ?

How many red ?

**B.** Count . _____8_____ ones = _____8_____

Count . _____5_____ tens = _____50_____

How many  does he have in all? _____58_____

## Ring the picture that shows the problem.

Karl has 33 . Then he

loses 21  in the sand.

How many  does he

have left?

-

-

## PRACTICE

**Use dimes and pennies to show.**
**Solve.**

1. Alex gets 32 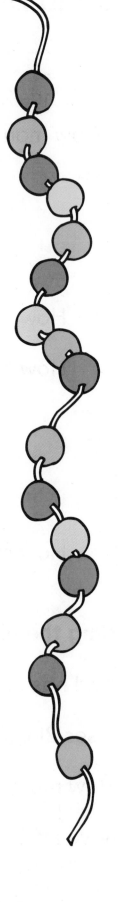 from Delia. Delia has 46 ⬭ now. How many more ⬭ does Delia have?_____ more ⬭

2. Delia needs 37 ⬭ for a 🔗. She has 68 ⬭. How many ⬭ will be left after she makes the 🔗?

   _____ ⬭

3. Alex uses 14 ⬭ for each 🔗 he makes. He makes 2 🔗. How many ⬭ does he use for both 🔗?

   _____ ⬭

4. Delia buys ⬭ for 32¢ a 🛍. She spends 96¢. How many 🛍 does she buy? _____ 🛍

# Underlining Needed Information

The  costs 25¢. The  costs 35¢.

Paul has 6 dimes. Can he buy 2  ?

**A.** Decide if you need all the information.
Draw a line under what you need.

<u>The  costs 25¢.</u>   The  costs 35¢.

<u>Paul has 6 dimes.</u> Can he buy 2 ?

**B.** Use the information you need. Solve the problem.

How much do 2  cost? ___50¢___

Can Paul buy 2  ? ___yes___

## Draw a line under the information you need.

Paul has 15 . He

has 24 . Then he gets

14 more . How many

 does he have now?

## PRACTICE

### Draw a line under the information you need. Solve.

1. Jen finds 30 🍁. She has 10 red 🍁. Hannah has 23 🍁. How many of Jen's 🍁 are not red?

   _____ 🍁

2. Bela has 21 white 🌼. He has 27 🍁. He finds 18 pink 🌼. How many more white than pink 🌼 does Bela have?

   _____ more white

3. Lee picks 42 🍒. He gives Sam 12 🍒. Kim has 31 🍒. How many 🍒 do Sam and Kim have?

   _____ 🍒

4. Bela puts 46 🍊 in his 📦. Hannah puts 29 🍊 in her 📦. Sam has 12 more 🍊 than Bela. How many 🍊 does Sam have?

   _____ 🍊

# Problem-Solving Practice

## Solve each problem.

1. Ling has 15 🐚. Carol has 27 🐚. Pete has 12 more 🐚 than Ling. How many 🐚 does Pete have? _____ 🐚

2. Min has 58 ⚪. Then she uses 23 to make a 📿. How many ⚪ does she have left? _____ ⚪

3. Keesha has 31 ⚪. Micah has 67 ⚪. How many more ⚪ does Micah have? _____ more ⚪

4. There are 24 🐦 in the field. Then 13 🐦 fly away. How many 🐦 are in the field now? _____ 🐦

# TEST-TAKING PRACTICE

## Ring the correct answer.

1. Tasha has 14 red .

   Tasha has 23 blue ⬤.

   Kita has 41 red ⬤.

   How many ⬤ does Tasha have?

   - 37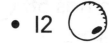
   - 55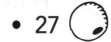

---

2. Al gives Sue 39 ⬤.

   Sue gives 12 ⬤ to Jian.

   How many ⬤ does Sue have now?

   - 12
   - 27

---

3. There are 18 🐦. Then

   12 fly away. How many 🐦

   are there now?

   - 6 🐦
   - 29 🐦

---

4. There are 36 🦆 on the pond.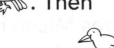

   Then 13 more 🦆 come.

   How many 🦆 are there now?

   - 23 🦆
   - 49 🦆